Hello out there!

ALL ABOUT MAPS

Catherine Chambers

Illustrated by Dave Cockcroft

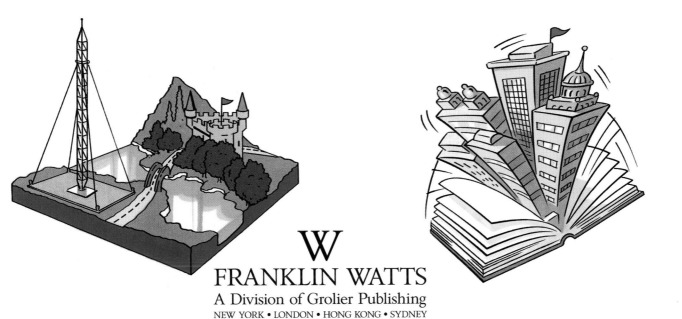

W
FRANKLIN WATTS
A Division of Grolier Publishing
NEW YORK • LONDON • HONG KONG • SYDNEY
DANBURY, CONNECTICUT

© Franklin Watts 1997
First American Edition 1998 by
Franklin Watts, A Division of Grolier Publishing
90 Sherman Turnpike, Danbury, CT 06816

Visit Franklin Watts on the Internet at:
http://publishing.grolier.com

Chambers, Catherine.
    All about maps / Catherine Chambers.
        p.   cm. -- (Hello out there!)
    Includes index.
    Summary: Discusses how and why we use maps and examines the many
different froms that they can take.
    ISBN 0-531-14471-2 (lib. bdg.)   0-531-15348-7 (pbk.)
    1. Maps--Juvenile literature. [1. Maps.] I. Title.
II. Series.
GA130.C455 1997
912--dc21   97-2396
                                                                      CIP
                                                                       AC

Series editor: Rachel Cooke
Series designer: Melissa Alaverdy
Designer: Robin Farrow
Picture research: Sarah Snashall

Printed in Belgium
Picture acknowledgments:
AKG London p. 22tr (Eric Lessing);
The Bridgeman Art Library p. 6bl (Bibliotheque Nationale, Paris);
The British Museum p. 16bl; Robin Farrow p. 12 both;
Robert Harding Picture Library p. 18b
London Regional Transport p. 15 (LRT Registered User No. 97/2613);
Science and Society Picture Library p. 25tr (NASA)
Science Photo Library pp. 19br (Simon Fraser),
21br (Philippe Plailly/Eurolios),
24bl (John Sanford), 26br (NASA); Steve Shott p. 11 both.

CONTENTS

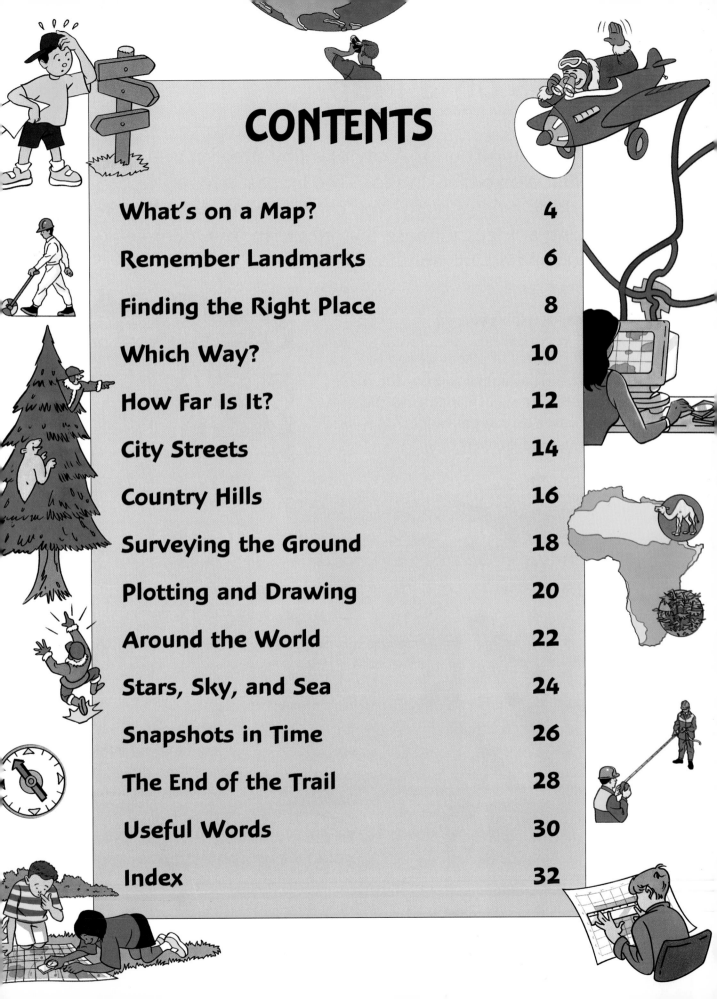

What's on a Map?

Where are you going to? A city or a tiny street in a city? What are you looking for? The longest river in the world or a tiny stream? You can find all these and more by looking at maps. Choose the right map, use it correctly, and you can find just about any place!

Up, Up, and Away!

Maps are pictures of places looked at from above. The higher you go, the more you can see. But what happens to the places you see as you get higher? Everything looks smaller!

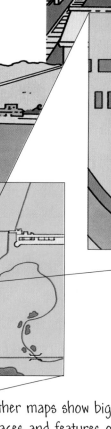

▲ Some maps show small areas. They have a few **features** marked in detail on them. It's like looking from a rooftop.

Other maps show big areas of land. They have lots more places and features on them, but they appear much smaller. It's like looking from high up in an airplane.

◀ Some maps show whole countries and continents. It's like looking at Earth from a **satellite** or spaceship!

Spot the Map!

You can use maps to find out information about a place. You can take them with you on a journey to help you find your way. In each case, you need to think carefully before choosing the map. Here are some very different types.

HELLO!

Maps and plans have existed for a very long time. Ancient Egyptians, whose civilization flourished between the 30th century and 10th century BC, thought maps were so important, they even had a god of plan-makers, whose name was Khonsa.

Treasure Trek 1

There's a treasure map on page 28 of this book! Follow the 12 clues through the book to find your prize. This is the first one: Start off where **X** marks the spot.

CITY PLAN

Bird-watching? This nature trail map will help.

Trail

ROAD MAP

▲ Sight-seeing? Buy a city street plan.

Skiing? ▶ This map will get you down the mountain.

SKI ROUTES

Clothes shop

Jewelers

Pharmacy

Newsagent

▲ Driving? Plan your **route** with this map.

◀ Shopping? Here's a plan of the mall.

Remember Landmarks

All around us are buildings, trees, or other objects that really stick out. Perhaps they are big. Maybe they are brightly colored. But they all help us to remember where we are. These are **landmarks**.

Signs and Symbols

Landmarks are often represented on maps. This means they are shown as **signs**, **symbols**, blocks of color, or patterns. Sometimes the symbols look like the real landmark. Others are harder to recognize.

Find these landmarks in this picture!

⚓	bridge	⬭	lake
🏰	castle	═	road
⌒ 250 ⌒ 220	hill	🗼	**transmitter**
		🌳	woodland

Landmarks are shown in different ways all over the world.

HELLO!

This map of Arabia and India was drawn by a European map-maker about 1,500 years ago. What landmarks can you see in it? Landmarks then were drawn much too big, but they showed what was important to people at the time.

What Do They Mean?

Signs, symbols, patterns, and colors can look confusing on a map. You need to look at the **key** to find out what they mean, so make sure you find the key on any map you use.

Key

— major road

— minor road

town

Color Coding

Keys often show the same feature but in different colors. Colors have become very important in mapmaking. They help you find the difference between the features that look the same.

On this map, two long roads go in the same direction. The green one is the quick main road. The red is slower. Different colors help you choose the road you want. ▼

The green areas on this map of Africa show where plants grow. The yellow areas show empty desert. ▼

Using color on maps like this is called **color coding**.

Treasure Trek 2

Look at the map above and find the color of the smaller roads. Follow the road with the same color on the treasure map.

Key

⬜ empty desert

🟩 plants growing

Finding the Right Place

Maps can cover a huge area. Thousands of things can be marked on them. So how do you find the spot you want? The easiest way is to use the **grid** of squares drawn on a map.

Over, Then Up

This supermarket plan is divided by a grid. The grid has numbers down one side and along the bottom.

The soft drinks are in square 2, 7. This is the **grid reference** number for the square. It lies 2 squares over, then 7 squares up. The fruit is in square 1, 1— 1 over and 1 up.

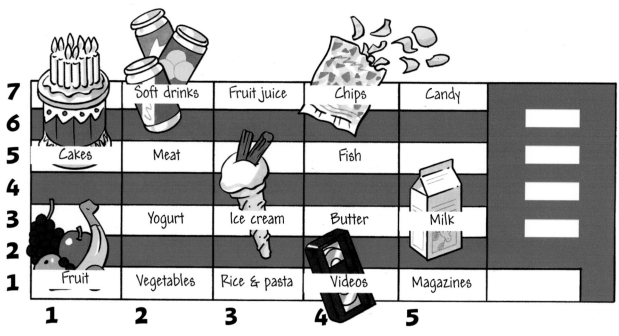

▲ Find the rest of your shopping using these grid numbers: **3,3; 1,5; 5,3; 4,1; 4,7.**

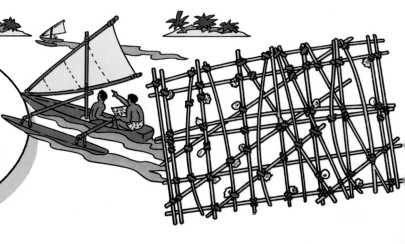

HELLO!
Seamen from the Marshall Islands in the Pacific Ocean used a grid map to help them sail to different islands. The grid was made of twigs, and shells placed in it showed the position of the islands.

Finding the Grid Reference

To find the grid reference you need on a map, you look at the index. The index shows the names of places in alphabetical order with their grid reference next to them.

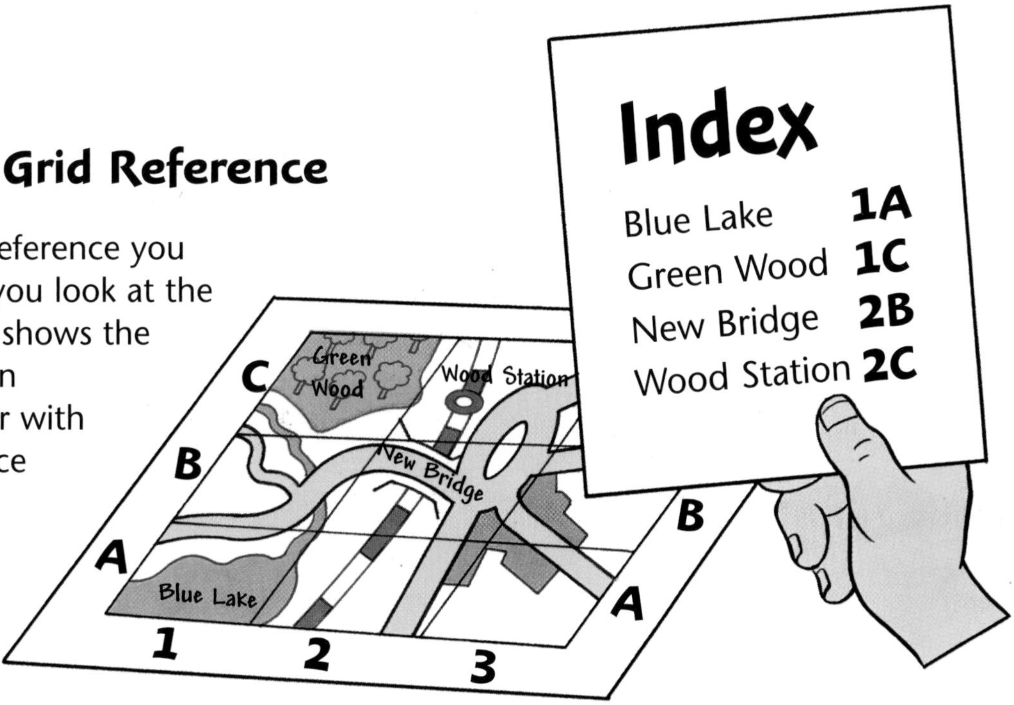

Some grid ▶ references use numbers and letters

Index

Blue Lake	**1A**
Green Wood	**1C**
New Bridge	**2B**
Wood Station	**2C**

Map labels: Green Wood, Wood Station, New Bridge, Blue Lake; grid letters C, B, A; grid numbers 1, 2, 3

Activity

Play a hop-scotch grid game with friends. Copy a grid and numbers on to the ground with chalk. Now throw a stone on to the grid. The first person to shout out the correct grid number where the stone lands hops and skips to the square to pick it up and hops back again. Then they can throw the stone.

Treasure Trek 3

You're following the small road on the treasure map. Stop when you get to the square 3B.

SPOT IT!

Grid lines can show direction, too. Usually, the lines going across show how far north or south you are. The lines going up and down show how far west or east you are.

Which Way?

You know where you are on a map. You know where you want to get to. **Compass points** on the map tell you the direction you need to go in. They show if your goal is north, south, east, or west of you. But look around you: It may be clear on the map, but which way is which in real life?

Following Directions

HI!

Landmarks can help you find your **bearings**—the direction you should be going in. For example, you are at the gate of this Fun Fair. The Rocket Ride is in front of you. Look at the map and find the landmark you can see: you are facing east (E on a **compass**).

You are here ▶

You are meeting a friend at the Super Splash. Use the compass points to follow these instructions:

▶ Go east until you reach the Thunder Rocket.
▶ Now go south to Buffalo Bill's Shooting Range.
▶ Turn east again and go as far as Count Dracula's Castle.

▶ Then go north over the Giant's Bridge.
▶ Turn west towards the Merry-Go-Round.
▶ Curve around to the north-west – you've found him.

Clever Compass

Landmarks can be confusing—one hill can look much like another. And sometimes you can't see any landmarks at all. Then you need a compass to help you find your bearings.

A compass has a magnetic needle that is always pulled to the north by the Earth's **magnetism**. Once you know where north is, you can follow the directions given by the map.

Rest a compass on something flat. The needle always points north—even though the dial might say something else (here it says south-west).

HELLO!

The earliest compass was called a lodestone. It was made out of a naturally magnetic rock. When it was suspended in the air, it hung in a line running from north to south.

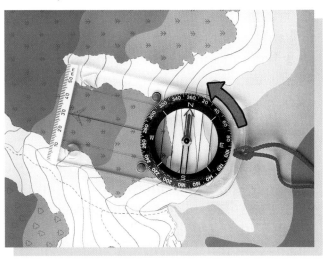

Twist the compass around—the needle doesn't move but the dial does. Now "N," or north, is at the top of the needle. All the other points on the compass are pointing in the right direction, too.

Treasure Trek 4

You've found the right square. Now go east until you get to the post office.

How Far Is It?

It is useful to know the distance between two places. Then you can work out how long it will take to get from one to the other. How can a map tell you the distance in real life?

Cutting Down to Size

Most maps are drawn to **scale**. This means everything on a map ends up in the same position as it is in real life. But it has all been shrunk by exactly the same amount to fit on the map. It is like shrinking a photograph. The scale marked on each map tells you how much things have been shrunk by.

Near or Far?

The distance between the hamburger stand and the snake shop is 2 inches. But it can't be 2 inches in real life. The scale tells you that on the map, 1 inch is the same as 20 feet in real life, so 2 inches on the map means 40 feet on the street.

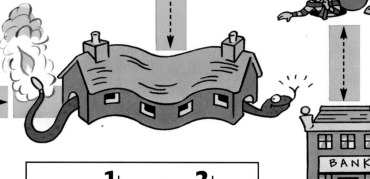

Use a ruler to work out the distances in real life between:
1. The juggler and the joke shop.
2. The manhole cover and the bank.
3. The fire and the fire station!

	1	2

Scale 1 inch = 20 feet

Honey, I Shrunk the Egg

Try using grids to draw an object to scale like this egg.

ACTIVITY

The road twisting around this page is drawn to the same scale as the town map: 1 inch = 20 feet. It is 3,702 feet long. Check that we are right. Carefully wind some string along the road. Cut the string where the road stops. Stretch your string out straight and measure it in inches. Now work out how long the road is in real life. Were we right?

This second box grid has been drawn half the size of the first – and so has the egg.

▲

The third is half the size of the second. The egg is smaller, but it is still the same shape.

Treasure Trek 5

Take your piece of string with you to the treasure map. Look at the scale. Measure 600 yards on your string. Go northwest this distance from the post office. Look out for a huge landmark to the west of your route.

Finish here

Start here

City Streets

Cities are huge. There are so many streets, and they all look the same. How can you possibly fit everything on a map?

The Key to the Maze

Many large cities are mapped in a book. Each area takes up a page. The map scale is large so that even tiny streets and features can be seen.

Bridge St. 34, A5
Eden Grove 3, H9
High Road 76, E6
Hill Road 45, B3
rket Pl. 55, M2

▲
You find the name of the street you need in the index at the back of the book. Next to it, you will see the page number, then the grid reference.

HELLO!
Some of the earliest maps were of towns and cities. A wall painting in Turkey that is over 8,000 years old shows a plan of streets and houses.

Other city maps are made in one huge piece. They are then folded until they are quite small. They, too, have an index.

INDEX

Under Your Feet

In many big cities, trains run through tunnels under the streets to help you get around. London has the oldest subway train system. It also has the oldest subway map.

Treasure Trek 6

Now go west to the nearest train station. Take the train and go two stations in a northeast direction, then get off.

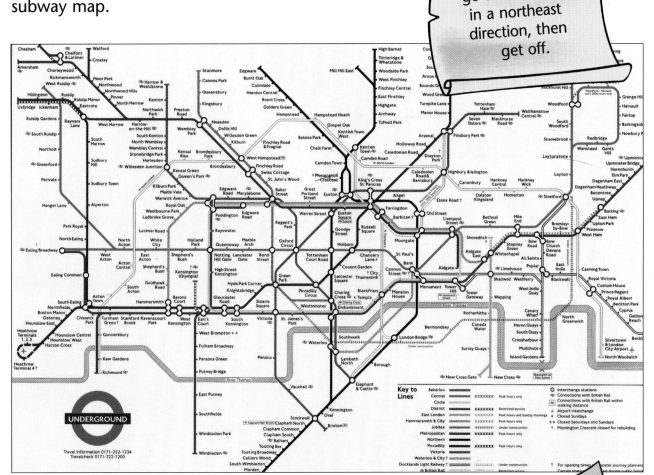

In 1933, mapmaker Henry Beck realized that London travelers didn't need to see all the bends in the underground railway track, or the exact distance between each station. All they needed was an idea of which direction each track took and to see the stations marked in the right order. This made the map much easier to read. This kind of map is called **topological**.

SPOT IT!

Well, someone's got to do it. Do what? Unblock the sewers and mend leaky water pipes under the ground. To do this, workers use maps of drains and water pipes.

Country Hills

On a country map you can find hills, valleys, rivers, marshlands, forests, and roads. Some people can even tell what kind of rock the land is made of—just by looking at the shapes of hills on a map! These maps are called **topographical**.

What Can You See?

Use the key on this map to help you find a pine forest, a village, a farm, marshland, and streams.

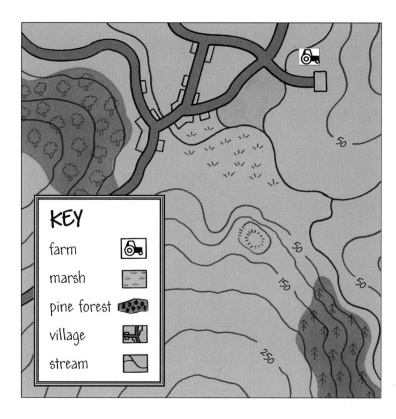

KEY

farm	
marsh	
pine forest	
village	
stream	

Hills and Valleys

There are lots of ways of showing hills. Sometimes, shading is used. At other times, a fringe of lines is drawn around the hill. This is known as hachuring. But the most accurate way of mapping hills is with **contour lines**.

This map of a valley in Mexico was drawn in 1583. It uses the a mapmaking style developed by the Aztecs, showing ranges of hills as green humped shapes. The blue shields are towns.

Shading used to show a hill

Fringe used to show a hill

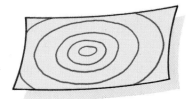

Contours used to show a hill

Lines of Equal Height

If you look at the map on the other page, you can see lots of brown lines. These are the contour lines. There are numbers on them. The brown lines join up places that are the same height. The numbers show how high these points are above **sea level**.

Height given in feet

The map above is of the hill shown left. You can work out the shape, size, and height of the hill just by looking at the map. Where the hill is steep, the contour lines are close together, because the height above sea level is increasing very quickly. Where the slope is gentle, the contour lines are farther apart.

HELLO!
Contour lines were first used in 1771. They were on a map that showed a part of France.

Fixing Sea Level

Sea level changes with the tides. But when we use the words "sea level" for maps, we mean a fixed level. This was worked out in Newquay in Cornwall, U.K. The highest and lowest levels were marked on the harbor wall. Sea level was fixed in between.

Treasure Trek 7

You are in the heart of the city, but there are still some green spaces. From your station, go into the nearest park. Follow the footpath near the station.

High Tide

Sea Level

Low Tide

Surveying the Ground

We call people who make maps **cartographers**. Their job can be roughly divided into two: first, gathering information, and second, putting it down on a map. The first part is called **surveying**.

What Goes on the Map?

Mapmakers have to decide what to put on the map. This is the first stage of surveying. They decide what features they need to show on it. Some of the features are places. Others are landmarks. Some are physical features, such as rivers and forests.

A Good View

Mapmakers need a good view of the area they want to map. A long time ago, they used to climb hills and tall buildings. This was to get information for maps with small details. But for nearly 100 years, photographs have been taken from low-flying airplanes, and more recently from satellites.

Satellite pictures, like this one of Washington DC, USA, are very useful in the process of surveying.

How Far Is It?

The second stage of surveying is measuring. Mapmakers measure the distance between features.

They could use a tape-measure.

They could measure by pacing.

What's the position?

Mapmakers also have to work out the position of each place or feature on the map. This means they have to work out the angle between one place or feature and another—there is some complex mathematics involved!

HELLO!

About 2,000 years ago there was a famous North African mapmaker named Ptolemy. He was one of the first mapmakers to use the angles and lengths of triangles to work out the exact positions of places.

Treasure Trek 8

Stop where the footpath meets a road. Turn left on to the road and move 200 yards along it.

They could use a trundle-wheel.

In fact, surveyors mostly use an electronic instrument to measure distances. It has an invisible **infrared light** beam that bounces off objects. This gives the exact distance from the surveyor to the object.

For large-scale maps, surveyors today often use a **theodolite** to measure angles accurately.

Plotting and Drawing

After mapmakers have surveyed the ground they want to map, they can begin the second part of their job: putting all the information they have gathered onto a map.

Let's Get Plotting

Now the information can be **plotted** on a map. All the surveyor's information is plotted: the features and the distances between them.

A Store of Information

Mapmakers make lists of all the information they have gathered. Nowadays, all the facts and figures can be fed into computers. The computer does not just store the information. It sorts it out, too.

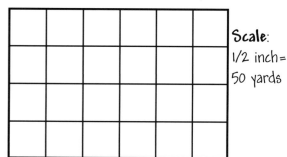

Scale: 1/2 inch= 50 yards

▲ First, the map grid has to be drawn to scale.

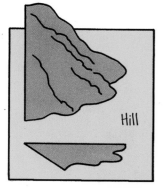

Hill

Bridge

Woods

Electricity towers

▲ All this information has been scaled down to fit on the map.

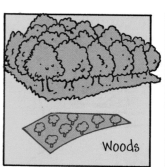

◀ The symbols are drawn to the same scale as the grid.

Drawing and Coloring

Some maps are still drawn and colored in by hand. But this is all done much more quickly on computer—no more coloring in!

At the press of a button, points plotted on the map can be joined up.

◄ Press another button and blocks of color fill in map outlines.

Maps for the Future

Mapmaking is changing all the time. Not all maps end up on paper. Many now stay on the computer screen. The screen does not have to show the whole map. It can be scrolled down, so that a new piece of the map appears when you need it.

HELLO!

The very latest maps are three-dimensional (3-D). They show the real shapes of features on a map that doesn't look flat. Soon there will be 3-D computer charts of airplane flight paths, helping air-traffic controllers to tell if one plane is going too close to another.

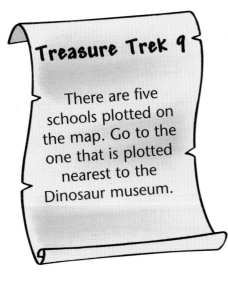

Treasure Trek 9

There are five schools plotted on the map. Go to the one that is plotted nearest to the Dinosaur museum.

Some people have computerized street maps in their cars. These help people find different routes when there is a traffic jam.

Around the World

Large-scale maps are useful because they show such a lot of detail. But why do we need maps of the world? What can we see on such a small scale? And how do we flatten out the globe?

The Earth Is a Sphere—But the Map Is Flat!

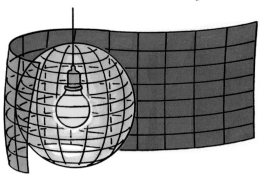

World maps are known as **projections**. This is because they are drawn as if a light is shone through a glass globe, projecting the shadows of the land areas onto paper.

Out of Shape

Projection maps are not strictly accurate. Flattening out the world pushes the land and sea areas out of shape. People argue about what is the best projection.

Mercator projection

▲

Most maps of the world follow the projection devised by the Dutchman Mercator over 400 years ago. His projection stretches out the land to the north and south of the globe so it shows North America larger than Africa—which isn't true!

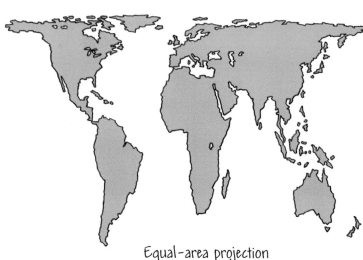

Equal-area projection

◀ Equal-area maps try to make the area of land occupied by continents match what it is in reality, but the land shapes are still not right.

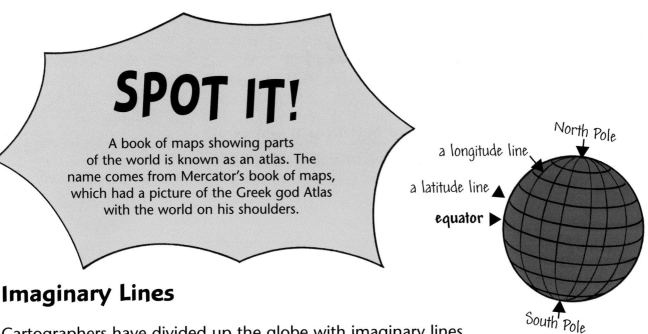

SPOT IT!

A book of maps showing parts of the world is known as an atlas. The name comes from Mercator's book of maps, which had a picture of the Greek god Atlas with the world on his shoulders.

a longitude line

a latitude line ▲

equator ▶

North Pole

South Pole

Imaginary Lines

Cartographers have divided up the globe with imaginary lines.
Latitude lines show how far north or south a place is.
Longitude lines show how far east or west it is. These are drawn as a grid on world maps.

World-Wise

World maps help us to compare different parts of the earth. You can compare climates, find out where different plants grow, see how people are spread through the world, and lots more. As with all maps, you have to choose the map you need. You still need a key to understand what you are looking at, too.

Treasure Trek 10

Make your way to the round dome of a building nearby. It has been flattened, so it is different from real life.

How cold is it in Iceland? Look at a world climate map. ▼

◀ Looking for mountain ranges and rivers? Find a world physical map.

highest
lowest

Want to ▶ know where in the world a country is? Look at a world political map.

coldest

warmest

Stars, Sky, and Sea

How do you find your way across the sea or in the air? How do you know where the stars are? You need to use charts. These are kinds of maps.

Stargazing

Before modern maps existed, people used the position of the stars and the Sun to work out where they were on the Earth and the oceans. Mapmakers in those times also had to be **astronomers** to draw up star charts. Sailors used these charts to navigate by.

Changing Skies

Mapping the stars is very difficult. Their positions are always changing as the Earth moves around the Sun.

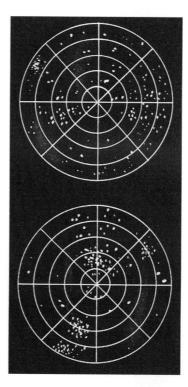

We divide the world in half with the equator. We call the half with the North Pole at its top the Northern **Hemisphere**.

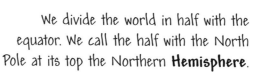

North Pole

◄ equator

South Pole

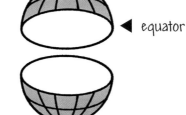

HELLO!

This might not be very useful to you now. But in the future, who knows? There are actually maps of the moon!

The other half, with the South Pole at its top, is the Southern Hemisphere. Star charts are also divided into hemispheres, as the stars you see depend on which half of the world you are in.

Across the Ocean

How deep is the ocean? Underwater scientists and sea captains often need to know. They use ocean charts to help them. Charts also show dangerous rocks and sandbanks under the surface, as well as buoys and harbor walls.

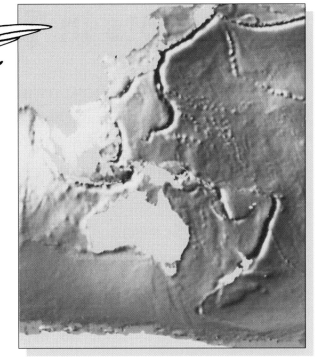

Once again, satellites are helping us make maps. This map was drawn from information gathered by satellite. It shows the varying depths of the earth's oceans.

Treasure Trek II

The Sun rises in the east and sets in the west. Follow the street that goes towards the setting Sun.

Depth Sounding

Ocean depths are measured by echo sounding, or **sonar**. A sound wave is sent to the ocean floor. Scientists measure the time it takes for the echo to come back. They know how fast sound travels through water, so they can work out the depth of the water that the echo went through.

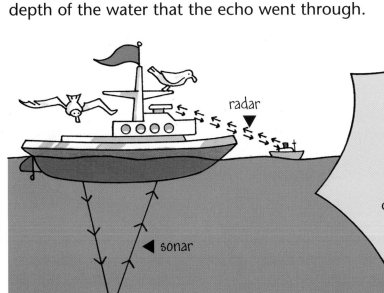

radar

sonar

SPOT IT!

Seamen also need to know where other ships are so they do not collide with them. Maps for this are now displayed on screens. Signals show where other ships are. Air-traffic controllers use a very similar system.

Snapshots in Time

Maps are drawn to show us information. But the information they give is taken at one particular time, like a snapshot. So maps get out of date, sometimes very quickly.

Changing Scenes

In a town, a new shopping mall might be built in a year. A cinema might close down. A map of the town drawn shortly before either of these events is now out of date.

Road maps often show roads still being built marked as dotted lines. This keeps the map up to date.

World maps date, too. Wars can change the border between two countries, as has happened recently in the former Yugoslavia.

Moving Maps

One type of map shows features that move all the time. These are weather maps. Weather changes without stopping, so the maps have to be constantly changed, too!

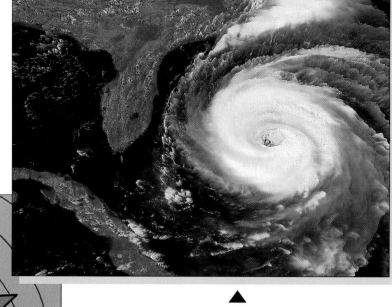

◀ This weather map shows the shape and movement of a huge storm.

▲ In this satellite picture, you can see the real storm clouds moving towards the coast of Florida.

What Maps Don't Tell

Maps don't tell us the whole story about a place, and a single map might not give you all the information that you need.

You can't see from the map how the coal is mined. It could be taken from deep under the ground. Or it could be mined on the surface.

It does not show how much coal is dug out from each mine every year.

Treasure Trek 12

Look down and you'll see some trash by your feet. The wind is blowing it along the pavement from the north. Follow it until you reach a new skyscraper.

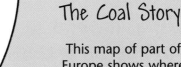

The Coal Story

This map of part of Europe shows where coal is mined.

Sometimes, mines spoil the land around them. But you can't see this on the map, either.

ACTIVITY

Ask an elderly person about the streets or countryside around you. What is there now that wasn't there, say, 50 years ago? Then redraw your local map without the new features.

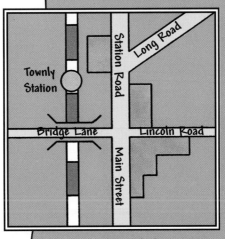

How it looked then.

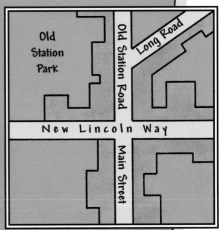

How it looks now.

The End of the Trail

You're nearly at the end of your trek. Just climb to the top of the skyscraper and you'll find a helicopter. This is your treasure. It will take you wherever you choose to go. Just find a place you want to go on a map.

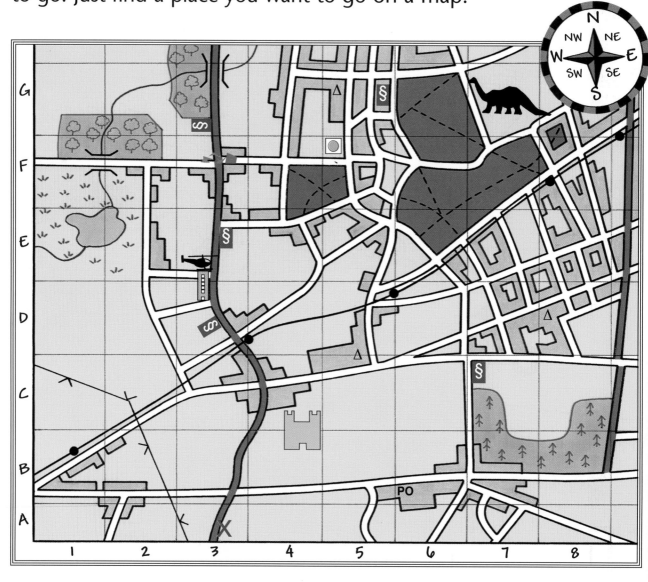

KEY
- **X** start here
- **PO** post office
- castle
- ●——● subway
- - - - - - footpath
- park
- § school
- △ museum
- dinosaur museum
- ◉ domed building
- helicopter
- trash
- skyscraper

Scale: 1 inch = 400 yards

Making Your Own Map

Try making a map of a small area—maybe a room, yard, or playground.

1. Start by noting down everything that you want to show on it.

2. Measure out the area. You can use a tape-measure or a measuring wheel. You can even measure it in strides.

3. Now decide on the scale of your map and draw up a grid (see pages 12-13). Draw the area you have measured to scale on the grid. Now you can begin to fill in the map.

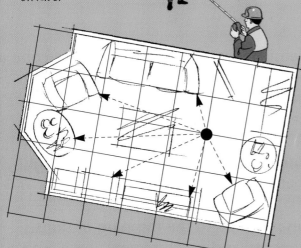

4. Stand at one point ●, and mark it on your map.

5. Measure the distance between you and each feature that you want to show.

6. Use a compass to tell you in which direction you are going from your starting point to your object.

7. Design a key for the features and details you want to map—you can have fun deciding which symbols and colors to use.

8. Use the information you have collected to mark each feature inside the outline area on your map.

KEY		
T.V.	?	
Round table	?	
Armchair	?	
Coffee table	?	
Sofa	?	

Useful Words

astronomer: someone who studies the features of the universe, such as stars.

bearing: the direction in which a place or point lies from another point or position. Bearings are often described by compass points.

cartographer: a person who makes maps.

color coding: using colors to tell the difference between features on a map.

compass: an instrument for finding direction. A compass has a magnetic needle which always points north. It is pulled that way by the earth's magnetism.

compass points: the directions on a compass. The four principal directions—north, south, east, and west—divide the circular dial of the compass into four equal parts.

contour lines: the lines on a topographical map which show the height and shape of land. The lines join up all points of the same or equal height.

equator: the imaginary line that circles the Earth halfway between the North and South Poles. The equator divides the earth into its Northern and Southern hemispheres.

features: the different details and objects, such as buildings, rivers, or country borders that are shown, or featured, on a map.

grid: a system of lines that cross each other that can be used for finding places on maps.

grid reference: the collection of numbers or letters and numbers that tells you where to find something on a map, using its grid.

hemisphere: the word used to describe a half of the world, such as the Northern Hemisphere. Hemi means half, so hemisphere is half a sphere.

infrared light: one of the parts of light that is invisible to the human eye.

key: a guide to the meaning of signs, symbols, and measurements on a map.

landmark: a large or colorful feature, such as a building or tree, that is easy to spot and to remember.

latitude lines: the imaginary lines that circle the earth, running parallel to the equator. They are used by cartographers to show how far north or south a place is.

longitude lines: the imaginary lines that circle the earth, each one passing through the North and South Poles. They are used by cartographers to show how far east or west a place is.

magnetism: the invisible force that pushes apart or pulls together certain magnetic materials, such as iron or steel. The earth has its own magnetism.

plot: (v.) to draw up a map and place information in the correct position on it.

projections: the name given to the way world maps are drawn flat, when the earth itself is sphere-shaped. There are several different projections, created using slightly different methods, so that the shape of land areas varies in each one.

route: a plan of a journey.

satellite: a man-made object which orbits, or circles, the earth in space.

scale: the amount a map has been shrunk from the area it is showing in real life to the area it occupies on the map. A measurement of the scale is shown on the key of the map.

sea level: the level of the sea when it is halfway between high tide and low tide. Heights on maps are always given as measurements starting from sea level. The height of land at sea level is 0.

signs: letters, pictures, or shapes that represent something else. On a map, signs are used to represent features.

sonar: a way of measuring the depth of the sea by bouncing sound off the seabed and listening for its echo.

surveying: measuring distances and features of the landscape. Surveying may be done to gather information for making maps, but it is also done for other reasons, for example, to draw up building plans.

symbols: pictures or patterns on a map that represent features.

theodolite: a surveryor's instrument used for measuring angles.

topographical: describes a map showing natural features, such as rivers and hills, as well as man-made features, such as roads.

topological: describes a map that shows features in the right order but does not give accurate measurements—it is not drawn to scale.

transmitter: a piece of equipment that sends out signals, such as radio and television signals. Transmitters are often very large and tall landmarks, so they are usually featured on maps.

Index